Onion Boy

Lance Jones

ISBN: 978-1-9993164-8-8

Dedication

I dedicate this book to my brothers and sisters: Rudolph, Westford, Norma, Arthur, Alma, and Stephen—the family who are also my friends. I hope this book inspires you to accomplish all the things that seem impossible and encourages you to never stop believing in your dreams.

Contents

Foreword

As you read Onion Boy, be prepare to be drawn into a journey of true friendship, courage, and self-discovery. This story from Lance G. Jones is more than just an adventure; it's a story that challenges every one who reads it to face their fearss, trust in their friends, and discover hidden abilities they may not aware of.

The story centers around a boy named Tyler, who finds himself connected to an unusual creature from another world, a creatue of light named Onion Boy. Together, they face not only physical challenges but also the daunting shadows of doubt and fear that put their friendship to test. Through trials, confrontations, and moments of vulnerability, Tyler learns that real courage comes from within and that true friendship can be a powerful light, even in the darkest times.

This story will inspire readers, both young and old, and encourage us that while we all face our own shadows, we never have to face them alone, the role of genuine friends is important. Lance G. Jones did a wonderful job of taking us - the readers on a whirlwind of emotions, blending moments of tension with warmth, laughter, and hope.

Acknowledgements

I would like to acknowledge my wife, Jennifer Jones, who has been my rock. I am also grateful to my children—Raphael, Jade, Nathanael, Lauren, Hurraine, Louise, and Charlene. They keep me entertained and young in spirit.

The Stranger in the Dark

Tyler lay on his bed, the blankets wrapped tightly around him as he stared at the ceiling. The darkness of his small room felt unusually heavy tonight. Every small sound—the ticking of the clock, the occasional creak in the floor—seemed to pulse louder, echoing in the silence. His heart beat rapidly, as if sensing something lurking just beyond the shadows.

It had been a terrible day, and it felt like there was no end to his frustration. At school, **Liam and his gang** had been relentless, taunting him and knocking his books to the ground. He'd told the teacher, but she'd given him a look that stung even more than Liam's words, one that seemed to say, *Not you again, Tyler.*

Things were no better at home. After dinner, his younger sister, **Naomi**, had once again caused trouble, snatching his favourite toy car and waving it tauntingly just out of reach. When he tried to grab it back, she tossed it to the floor with a look of pure innocence. Mum had rushed in, taking Naomi's side, as always.

"Tyler, how could you?" she'd scolded, barely sparing him a glance before taking Naomi away, comforting her as if he'd done something terrible. He'd tried to explain, but she'd only given him that same tired, disappointed look.

"Just go to bed, Tyler," she said, dismissing him.

He glanced at Dad, hoping for a hint of sympathy or even a glance, but Dad was too absorbed in his computer, eyes glued to the glow of his screen. The numbers and charts Tyler didn't understand seemed more important than anything else—especially Tyler.

Now, here he was, lying in bed, his frustration swirling with the loneliness he tried so hard to ignore. Why did no one ever take his side? Why did everyone seem to assume he was always at fault?

He turned over, clenching his fists, feeling the resentment bubbling up. He'd had enough. As his anger faded to exhaustion, he squeezed his eyes shut, willing himself to just fall asleep and forget the day.

But sleep didn't come. Tyler tossed and turned, feeling a strange prickling sensation along his skin, as if something was watching him. He tried to ignore it, but the feeling only grew stronger. Hesitantly, he opened his eyes.

At the foot of his bed, a soft glow flickered—small at first, like the dim glow of a nightlight, but brightening steadily. His breath hitched as he stared, frozen in place.

It was a head.

Shaped like a **shallot**, its smooth, slightly tapered surface was unlike anything he had ever seen. The creature had **piercing blue eyes** that shone brightly, gazing at him with an intensity that froze Tyler in place. Instead of a nose, there was only smooth skin beneath the eyes, and a pair of thin, blue lips, tightly pursed, adding a hint of mystery to the creature's expression.

The creature's colours shifted—a swirling, muted green, as though mirroring the loneliness and confusion Tyler felt.

But Tyler didn't feel curious—only a rising terror. He opened his mouth, and a terrified scream tore from his throat, shattering the silence. His eyes stayed locked on the floating head as it stared back, unblinking, its colours flickering into an alarmed red-orange.

Footsteps thundered down the hallway, and within seconds, his parents burst into his room. His mum, her face pale, rushed to his side, pulling him close as he clutched her arm with trembling hands.

"What's wrong, Tyler?!" Mum's voice was shaky, and she smoothed his hair, her hands gentle but frantic. "Did you have a nightmare?"

"It was right there! I saw it!" Tyler pointed to the foot of the bed, but the glow, the piercing blue eyes, the shallot-shaped head—everything was gone, swallowed by the darkness.

Dad flicked on the light, casting a warm glow over the room. He looked around, his gaze scanning every corner. "There's nothing here, Tyler. Are you sure you weren't just dreaming?"

Tyler shook his head vigorously, his heart pounding. "No, Dad, it was right there! This… this thing… it had a head like an onion, and it was glowing, and it looked at me…"

His parents exchanged a quick, worried glance. Mum's arms tightened around him. "It's alright, sweetheart. Sometimes our minds play tricks on us, especially when we're tired."

"But it felt real," Tyler whispered, his voice barely a whimper.

His mum kissed his forehead, pulling him close again. "You're safe now, love. We're right here."

Dad knelt by the bed, giving him a steady, reassuring look. "Tell you what—we'll leave the hallway light on tonight. If you see anything again, just call us, okay?"

Tyler nodded slowly, though a part of him felt they hadn't understood at all. They hadn't seen those piercing blue eyes or felt the warm yellow glow that had spread over him. But he kept quiet, gripping his mother's arm as she settled him back under the covers.

They stayed with him until he drifted into an uneasy sleep, his mind filled with the memory of the strange creature and its intense, otherworldly gaze.

An Unexpected Visitor

The next morning, Tyler felt as though he was moving through fog. The image of that strange head with its piercing blue eyes lingered in his mind. As he got ready for school, his parents seemed to have already forgotten the incident, treating his story as nothing more than a bad dream. But to Tyler, it had felt real—too real.

At school, he tried to push the memory aside, but his thoughts kept drifting back. He could still feel the creature's colours shifting, the green and purple dancing in the dark. He wondered if he'd see it again or if it had been some kind of one-time encounter.

By the time he got home, his nerves were frayed. Every sound seemed to startle him, and his eyes kept flicking to the shadows in each corner of the room, searching for any sign of the strange figure. He managed to eat dinner without incident, though Naomi kept pestering him about being "jumpy" and acting weird.

Their parents didn't seem to notice, too engrossed in their own routines to pay much attention.

After dinner, Tyler went to his room, closing the door quietly behind him. He sat on his bed, his heart pounding. Part of him hoped the creature wouldn't return. But another part of him—one he barely wanted to admit—was curious.

The minutes ticked by, and as the house settled into silence, Tyler's eyelids grew heavy. He drifted off, slipping into a light, restless sleep.

But he didn't stay asleep for long.

Sometime around midnight, he was jolted awake by a familiar feeling—that unmistakable sensation of being watched. Heart pounding, he opened his eyes, and there it was again.

The head hovered at the foot of his bed, its soft glow illuminating the room just enough to reveal its unusual features. Shaped like a shallot, its smooth, tapered skin glowed faintly in the dark, and its blue eyes shone, both intense and gentle.

Tyler froze, his breath caught in his throat. But this time, he didn't scream. He just lay there, unable to look away.

The creature's colours shifted slowly, blending into a calming shade of pale blue. Tyler could almost feel it trying to communicate something, a sense of peace that eased the tension in his chest.

"What... what are you?" Tyler whispered, barely daring to speak.

The creature tilted its head slightly, its eyes narrowing in what looked like curiosity. Its colours changed again, this time swirling with a soft yellow—almost as if it was... happy?

Tyler felt a strange urge to reach out, his fingers trembling. The creature seemed to understand, floating closer until it hovered just inches away from his hand. Its glow brightened slightly, a warm orange-yellow that wrapped around his fingers like a soft blanket.

For a moment, all of Tyler's fear vanished. He felt something he hadn't felt in a long time: acceptance. As if, somehow, this creature understood him in a way no one else could. He let his fingers relax, feeling the warmth of its glow.

"You don't... want to hurt me, do you?" Tyler asked, his voice a little stronger now.

The creature blinked, its blue eyes softening, and its colours shifted to a reassuring green. Tyler felt his heart slow down as he looked into its eyes, almost like looking into a mirror of his own feelings. The creature was scared, too—maybe even lonely, just like him.

Without another word, the creature tilted its head again, then slowly floated back towards the shadows, fading into the darkness just as it had the night before.

Tyler sat there in silence, his hand still outstretched, feeling a strange emptiness as he watched it disappear. For the first time, he found himself wanting it to stay.

"Wait!" he whispered, but the creature was already gone, leaving only the memory of its warm, shifting colours in his mind.

Tyler lay back down, his heart racing, as questions filled his head. What was it? Why had it come back? And why, he wondered, did he suddenly feel less alone than he had in a long time?

As he drifted back to sleep, he realised he wanted to see the creature again.

Onion Boy Communicates

Tyler barely slept the night after Onion Boy's second visit. His mind buzzed with questions, and he found himself longing for answers. The creature was strange and mysterious, yet somehow comforting. Tyler had never felt such a mix of fear and fascination; he couldn't stop thinking about those piercing blue eyes and the warmth that had wrapped around his hand.

The next night, as the house settled into quiet once more, Tyler lay wide awake, his gaze fixed on the foot of his bed. He waited, his heart thudding in his chest, hoping that Onion Boy would return.

Just as he was about to give up, a soft glow appeared.

There it was again—the head shaped like a shallot, with those unblinking blue eyes and that smooth, faintly glowing skin. Tyler gasped, feeling a blend of surprise and relief. But before he could speak, Onion Boy leaned closer and let out a soft, sharp *hiss* that sent a chill down Tyler's spine. The creature's colours flickered, glowing red-orange, and then—just as suddenly as he'd appeared—he vanished, dissolving back into the darkness.

Tyler's heart raced as he sat up, breathless. *What had just happened?* Had he frightened Onion Boy? Or was the hiss some sort of warning? Tyler wasn't sure, but he couldn't shake the feeling of those eyes staring into his.

Several moments passed, and Tyler began to doubt he'd see Onion Boy again. He lay back on his pillow, torn between wanting to call out and fearing he'd scare the creature off entirely.

Then, to his surprise, the glow returned, but this time it was softer, almost tentative. Onion Boy reappeared, his colours shifting to a calming shade of pale blue. Tyler took a deep breath, feeling his fear fade. He sensed that Onion Boy was reaching out, wanting to communicate.

"Are you… trying to tell me something?" Tyler whispered.

At that moment, Onion Boy's eyes locked onto his, and a soft glow radiated from his head, spreading across the room. Suddenly, shapes and colours began to form on Tyler's bedroom wall. Tyler's eyes widened as he watched the glow transform, taking the shape of faint images—images from his own mind.

Tyler gasped as he saw memories flickering on the wall: images of Naomi teasing him, his parents scolding him, and the loneliness he'd felt after so many rough days. The creature's glow darkened briefly, tinged with a shade of green, as if it understood the sadness and isolation that filled Tyler's thoughts.

"Can you… read my mind?" Tyler asked, his voice barely a whisper.

Onion Boy's colours shifted to a reassuring yellow, and a new set of images appeared on the wall. Tyler watched, captivated, as Onion Boy projected his own world—a landscape of strange, shimmering lights, dense forests, and other beings similar to him, each glowing and floating in a world of colours. The scene was otherworldly, both beautiful and mysterious, and Tyler couldn't look away.

But just as the vision became clearer, a dark shadow appeared on the wall, slinking through Onion Boy's projected world like a growing storm. Onion Boy's colours changed to a sharp, anxious red, and the image on the wall flickered, distorting before it vanished altogether.

Tyler stared at Onion Boy, his pulse quickening. "Is that… something dangerous?"

Onion Boy's colours softened to a deep purple, and he drifted back slightly, as if unsure of how much to reveal. But Tyler understood that whatever shadow had appeared was something threatening, something that had chased Onion Boy here to his world.

"It's okay," Tyler said, trying to sound braver than he felt. "You can stay here. I'll… I'll keep your secret."

Onion Boy's colours brightened to a warm yellow, and he gave the faintest hint of a nod. For the first time, Tyler felt as though he'd made a friend—a real friend who understood him. As Onion Boy faded back into the darkness, Tyler realised that he couldn't wait to see him again, no matter what mysteries lay ahead.

Onion Boy Goes to School

Tyler couldn't stop thinking about Onion Boy. Every night, he waited for the familiar glow to appear in his room, and Onion Boy never failed to return, each time bringing a comforting warmth Tyler had never known before. But tonight, Onion Boy had something different in mind.

It was early morning, just before sunrise, and Tyler was startled awake by a soft glow at the foot of his bed. He sat up, rubbing his eyes, and there was Onion Boy, floating patiently with his soft blue glow.

"Hey," Tyler whispered, surprised. "It's not even night-time."

Onion Boy's colours flickered to a warm yellow as if amused, then shifted to a bright, curious green. Tyler felt a mix of excitement and dread. He had a feeling that Onion Boy wanted to follow him to school.

"You want to come with me, don't you?" Tyler murmured, almost laughing at the thought.

Onion Boy bobbed slightly in response, his colours brightening with enthusiasm. Tyler bit his lip. It was risky—who knew what could happen if someone else saw Onion Boy? But something inside him was thrilled at the idea of sharing his secret with the world, even if just a little bit.

"Alright," Tyler whispered. "But you have to be really, really careful. You can't just… glow everywhere."

Onion Boy's colours dimmed to a muted green, as if signalling he'd keep himself hidden. Tyler gave him a reassuring nod and hurried to get ready for the day, stuffing his school bag with books and lunch, all while glancing over his shoulder to see if Onion Boy was still floating quietly behind him.

As he walked to school, Onion Boy hovered beside him, invisible to anyone who passed by. Tyler could feel the faint warmth of his silent friend following him like a shadow.

When they finally reached school, Tyler turned to Onion Boy. "You have to stay hidden in my bag, alright? Don't peek out. Just… stay quiet."

Onion Boy tilted his head, his colours turning to a patient, soft blue. Tyler couldn't help but smile as he slipped Onion Boy into his bag, pulling the zipper just enough to keep him covered but with enough space to see out if he wanted.

The first few classes went smoothly. Tyler tried to focus, but he could feel Onion Boy's presence, the warmth seeping through his bag like a little secret. It made him feel braver, less alone.

But everything changed during the science lesson.

Mr. Foster, the science teacher, was droning on about photosynthesis, his voice a slow, monotonous hum that lulled most of the class into daydreams. Tyler, lost in his own thoughts, almost forgot about Onion Boy until he heard a strange, soft *hiss*.

Tyler's eyes widened. He glanced down at his bag, barely lifting the zipper. A soft, yellow glow seeped through, and Onion Boy's head peered out, his colours a playful shade of purple and blue.

"No, no… get back in," Tyler whispered, but Onion Boy's glow only brightened.

Suddenly, a girl next to him gasped, looking directly at Tyler's bag. Tyler froze, snapping the zipper shut just as Mr. Foster turned around, his brows furrowed.

"Tyler, is there something you'd like to share with the class?" Mr. Foster's voice had a sharp edge, and Tyler felt a flush creep up his cheeks.

"Uh… no, sir," he stammered.

But Onion Boy had other plans. The little creature, perhaps feeling curious or playful, managed to wriggle free again, poking his glowing head out of the bag just as Mr. Foster turned back to the board.

The glow intensified, casting faint colours across Tyler's desk. Tyler watched, horrified yet amused, as Onion Boy's colours changed—deep purples, flashes of orange, and a hint of mischievous red.

Mr. Foster's voice cut off mid-sentence. "Tyler!"

Tyler jumped, hastily covering his bag, but it was too late. A faint glow escaped, casting a streak of orange across his desk. A few other students noticed, their eyes widening as they whispered to each other, unsure if they'd really seen a glowing onion-like creature or if it was a trick of the light.

"Bring your bag here, Tyler," Mr. Foster commanded, his eyes narrowing.

Tyler's heart raced. If Mr. Foster saw Onion Boy, who knew what would happen? But he couldn't keep the creature hidden forever. Trying to think quickly, Tyler reached into his bag and, in a sudden burst of bravery, tapped Onion Boy's head lightly, silently willing him to disappear.

And just like that, Onion Boy's glow vanished. Tyler let out a shaky breath, lifting his now completely dark bag as Mr. Foster inspected it. He opened the bag, flipping through books and papers, but found nothing out of the ordinary.

Mr. Foster frowned, clearly unsatisfied. “I don’t know what you’re playing at, Tyler, but pay attention. No more disruptions.”

“Yes, sir,” Tyler mumbled, relief flooding over him as he returned to his desk.

As soon as class ended, Tyler rushed to the bathroom, unzipping his bag the moment he was alone. Onion Boy reappeared, his colours flashing with an impish blue and purple, as if he were silently laughing at the whole ordeal.

“You nearly got us both in trouble!” Tyler whispered, but he couldn’t help the grin spreading across his face. Onion Boy’s glow softened to a gentle, innocent yellow, and Tyler shook his head, chuckling. “Alright, you win. But you have to be more careful.”

Onion Boy’s colours turned to a warm green, and Tyler felt his heart warm in response. Somehow, the little creature’s presence made him feel braver, more certain of himself than he ever had before.

As they left the bathroom, Tyler wondered what new mischief awaited him with Onion Boy by his side. Whatever happened, he knew one thing for certain: life was a lot more interesting—and a lot less lonely—with his glowing friend in tow.

Nosey Mary

The rest of the day at school passed in a haze for Tyler. He couldn't stop glancing at his bag, feeling both relieved and amused by Onion Boy's mischievous glow during science. But he hadn't expected anyone to notice, especially not **Mary**.

Mary was sharp—almost too sharp. She was the type who always had her hand up with an answer before anyone else and never missed a detail. Tyler usually tried to stay out of her way, but today was different. As the final bell rang and students gathered their things, Mary caught his eye with a knowing look.

"You've got something in there, haven't you?" she said, nodding toward his bag.

Tyler forced a laugh, tucking his bag close to his side. "What are you talking about?"

Mary narrowed her eyes. "I saw it. That glow coming from your bag. It was strange… like something alive."

Tyler's heart thudded. He tried to keep his expression neutral, shrugging casually. "You must have imagined it."

But Mary wasn't easily convinced. She leaned in, her eyes searching his face. "I didn't imagine anything. And I'm going to find out what you're hiding, Tyler."

Tyler gulped, trying to think of a way to shake her off. "There's nothing to find out, Mary," he muttered, slinging his bag over his shoulder. "Just… let it go, alright?"

As he turned to leave, he caught a glimpse of a faint blue glow coming from inside his bag. His stomach dropped. Onion Boy was getting restless again.

Mary's eyes widened, catching the faint glimmer just before it disappeared. She gasped, moving to block his way. "You're hiding something! What is it? Is it… something magical?"

Tyler looked around the hallway, noticing a few other students still lingering nearby. He leaned closer, his voice barely a whisper. "Look, even if there was something, I couldn't tell you. And it's… it's private."

Mary crossed her arms, not backing down. "Then let me see it. I swear I won't tell anyone. I just want to know."

Tyler hesitated, his mind racing. He knew he couldn't keep Onion Boy a complete secret, not if Mary was already suspicious. But he also knew Onion Boy's presence was something fragile, something he didn't fully understand yet himself. Still, Mary's determined gaze told him she wouldn't let this go.

"Fine," he whispered finally. "But not here. And you have to swear—*swear*—you'll keep it secret."

Mary's eyes sparkled with excitement as she nodded eagerly. "Alright. I swear. I won't tell a soul."

They made their way to a quiet spot outside, behind the row of trees by the school's fence. Tyler looked around, making sure no one was watching. Mary stood expectantly, arms crossed, her eyes fixed on his bag.

"Alright, Onion Boy," Tyler whispered, opening the bag a crack. "But be careful, alright?"

Slowly, a soft, warm glow began to seep out of the bag. Mary's eyes widened as Onion Boy's head appeared, his shallot-shaped head tilting to take her in. His colours shifted from a deep purple to a curious yellow, and Tyler could see the wonder on Mary's face.

"It's… it's real!" Mary whispered, her voice a mix of awe and disbelief. She reached out, her hand hovering near Onion Boy, her fingers trembling.

Onion Boy looked at her with his piercing blue eyes, his colours brightening to a playful orange. He leaned forward, giving a soft hiss that made Mary jump slightly.

"Careful, he doesn't like surprises," Tyler said, suppressing a grin.

Mary kept her hand still, watching as Onion Boy's colours flickered between green and blue, as if he were sizing her up. "He's… he's beautiful," she whispered.

Tyler felt a warm pride bloom inside him. "Yeah, he is. But you have to keep him a secret. I don't know where he came from, or… what he is exactly, but he's special."

Mary nodded, her eyes never leaving Onion Boy. "Don't worry. I won't tell anyone. But… how did you find him?"

Tyler glanced at Onion Boy, who floated closer, his colours dimming to a soft green, as if echoing the same question. "He just… showed up. I saw him one night in my room. And he… he can show me things—like memories. And sometimes he can see into my thoughts."

Mary's eyebrows shot up. "He can read minds?"

"Well, sort of. He can… sense things," Tyler explained. "And he can project things on the wall, like pictures of his world."

Mary's eyes shone with wonder. "What's his world like?"

Tyler hesitated, unsure how to explain the strange, vibrant images Onion Boy had shown him. "It's… hard to describe. It's full of colours, different from anything we've got here. And there are… other things like him, I think."

Onion Boy's colours shifted to a darker shade, tinged with a faint red. Tyler noticed and felt a pang of worry. He wasn't sure how much Onion Boy wanted him to share.

"Maybe we should get going," he said, glancing at Mary. "It's almost time to head home."

Mary nodded, reluctantly pulling her hand back. "Alright. But Tyler… you have to promise to let me see him again. He's amazing."

Tyler gave her a small smile. "We'll see. But remember—you can't tell anyone."

Mary grinned. "Not a soul."

With one last look at Onion Boy, she walked off, casting glances over her shoulder as if to make sure she hadn't imagined it all.

As Tyler watched her go, he felt a strange mix of relief and unease. He'd let someone else in on his secret, someone who seemed fascinated by Onion Boy but who might have her own reasons for staying close. Still, Onion Boy seemed content, his colours shifting to a calm, warm yellow as he slipped back into the bag.

Tyler zipped the bag up gently, a grin spreading across his face. He wasn't sure if he could fully trust Mary, but he had a feeling his life had just become a lot more interesting.

Tyler's Jealousy

Over the next few days, Onion Boy's presence became a quiet but comforting part of Tyler's life. He enjoyed having him nearby, feeling a strange sense of security whenever that soft glow flickered beside him.

However, Tyler couldn't ignore Mary's growing curiosity. Since the day she'd seen Onion Boy, Mary had found every excuse to talk to Tyler, asking questions and pressing him for details about Onion Boy's world. Tyler didn't mind, but he started to feel a prickle of something he hadn't expected: jealousy.

One afternoon, as they walked home from school, Mary spotted Onion Boy floating just above Tyler's shoulder, his colours a warm yellow. She grinned, quickening her step to walk beside them.

“Hi, Onion Boy,” she said cheerfully, giving him a small wave. Onion Boy turned to her, his colours shifting to a happy orange, and he tilted his head in greeting.

Tyler forced a smile, feeling a strange pang. *Why was Onion Boy so cheerful around her?* He shook the thought away, trying to ignore the feeling.

“Has he shown you anything new?” Mary asked, looking at Tyler with wide, eager eyes.

“Not… really,” Tyler said, his voice quieter than he intended. “He’s been around a lot, though. Just, you know, hanging out.”

But Onion Boy seemed to sense Mary’s excitement, and his colours began to shift, swirling into deep purples and blues. Tyler felt a twinge of annoyance. Onion Boy usually used those colours to show his playfulness around him, not anyone else.

“Hey, maybe he could show me something about his world?” Mary asked hopefully.

Tyler hesitated. *This was his secret, his friend.* He didn’t want to share every part of Onion Boy’s world with someone else, even if it was Mary. “I’m not sure… he doesn’t always want to show things.”

“Oh, come on, Tyler,” Mary said, flashing him a grin. “He doesn’t mind, do you, Onion Boy?”

Onion Boy floated between them, his colours flickering thoughtfully. He gave a soft hiss and faded out of sight, leaving only the memory of his glow lingering between them. Mary blinked, surprised, and looked at Tyler.

"Oh… I didn't mean to upset him," she said, a frown creasing her brow.

"It's fine," Tyler mumbled, his tone sharper than he intended. "Maybe he's just tired of all the questions."

Mary's face fell, and Tyler immediately regretted his words. But before he could apologise, Onion Boy reappeared, his colours shifting to a deep green, looking directly at Tyler with an almost disappointed expression.

Mary took a step back, glancing between Onion Boy and Tyler. "Maybe I should go. I… didn't mean to intrude or anything."

Without waiting for an answer, Mary turned and walked down the street, casting one last glance at Onion Boy before disappearing around the corner.

Tyler felt a pang of guilt as he watched her go. Onion Boy's colours softened to a sad blue, and he hovered closer to Tyler, his gaze questioning.

"I just… don't want to lose you to someone else, alright?" Tyler murmured, surprised at his own words. He'd never thought of himself as a jealous person, but something about Onion Boy's interactions with Mary stirred feelings he couldn't shake.

Onion Boy tilted his head, his colours shifting to a reassuring yellow. He floated closer, his glow brightening softly, almost as if he were trying to ease Tyler's mind.

"I know," Tyler said, giving him a small smile. "I just… want you to stay around."

Onion Boy's glow brightened to a warm orange, and Tyler felt a sense of relief wash over him. Maybe Onion Boy would always be his friend, no matter who else he met along the way.

As they walked home together, Tyler's jealousy faded, replaced by the quiet comfort of knowing that Onion Boy was his to keep, for as long as he needed him.

The Mysterious Shadow

Tyler felt a new sense of security with Onion Boy by his side. Every evening after school, they'd walk home together, Onion Boy floating beside him, fading in and out of sight whenever someone came near. Tyler had never had a friend quite like him—a friend who always seemed to understand.

But as the days passed, strange things began to happen.

One night, Tyler was lying in bed, drifting off to sleep, when he felt a sudden chill. The air felt heavier, like a dense fog pressing down on him. He opened his eyes, his heart pounding as he noticed Onion Boy glowing faintly near the window, his colours dim and wavering in shades of dark grey and green.

"Onion Boy?" Tyler whispered, sitting up. "What's wrong?"

Onion Boy's glow flickered, his head turning slowly to the far corner of the room. Tyler followed his gaze, feeling his skin prickle with dread. In the shadows, something stirred—something darker than the usual dimness of night.

A shape, like a moving shadow, seemed to flicker in and out of existence. Tyler felt his breath catch, and Onion Boy hissed softly, his colours deepening to a fearful shade of grey-black.

The shadow moved closer, taking on a twisted, shifting form, as if it were made of smoke. Tyler's heart raced as he clutched his blanket, not daring to move.

"W-what is that?" Tyler whispered, his voice barely audible.

Onion Boy floated closer to him, his glow becoming a protective shade of red and orange. The shadow lingered, its form flickering and shifting, as though sizing them up. Tyler felt a chill seep through him, an unmistakable feeling that whatever this was, it meant them harm.

Suddenly, the shadow darted forward, and Onion Boy surged into action, his glow intensifying to a blazing red. He floated between Tyler and the shadow, his colours flashing in a warning.

The shadow hesitated, retreating slightly as Onion Boy's glow grew brighter. But even as it moved back, Tyler could feel its presence lingering, as though it were waiting, biding its time.

Finally, the shadow dissolved, vanishing into the darkness as quickly as it had appeared. The room fell silent, but the air felt thick with an unspoken threat.

Tyler looked at Onion Boy, his heart still racing. "What... was that?"

Onion Boy's colours softened to a deep blue, and he floated closer, his gaze sad and almost apologetic. Tyler reached out, his hand brushing against Onion Boy's faint warmth.

"Is it something… from your world?" Tyler asked.

Onion Boy's colours shifted to a muted green, then a worried purple, as if struggling to communicate something complicated. Slowly, he projected an image onto the wall—a faint vision of his world, a place filled with shimmering lights and peaceful colours. But then, the image shifted, showing a dark shape lurking in the background, similar to the shadow that had just appeared.

Tyler watched, his chest tight. "So it followed you… here?"

Onion Boy's colours flickered to a sad grey, confirming Tyler's worst fear. The creature—whatever it was—had come from Onion Boy's world, and it seemed intent on finding him.

Tyler felt a surge of protectiveness. He didn't fully understand what was going on, but he knew one thing: he couldn't let anything happen to Onion Boy. Not now, not ever.

"We'll figure this out," he whispered, trying to sound braver than he felt. "You're safe here. I won't let it get you."

Onion Boy's glow warmed to a soft yellow, and he gave Tyler a reassuring nudge. For a moment, Tyler felt the heaviness of the encounter lift, replaced by a renewed sense of determination. Whatever this shadow was, they'd face it together.

As Tyler lay back down, Onion Boy stayed close, his glow a protective halo in the dark. Tyler knew that his life had just grown more complicated, but he couldn't imagine it any other way. Because for the first time, he had a friend worth fighting for.

Tyler's Decision

The encounter with the shadow left Tyler shaken. For days, he couldn't stop replaying the moment in his mind—the eerie silence, the twisting darkness, and Onion Boy's fierce, protective glow. But it was the shadow's presence that lingered with him, an unspoken threat he couldn't ignore.

At school, Tyler struggled to concentrate. Even Mary noticed his distraction, asking if he was alright. But Tyler brushed her off, reluctant to reveal the danger that had followed Onion Boy into his life. Besides, he had no idea how to explain it.

That night, as he lay in bed, Tyler noticed Onion Boy hovering beside him, his colours dim and thoughtful, as if lost in his own worries. The usual warmth between them felt distant, and Tyler realised that Onion Boy was afraid too. For all his silent bravery, even Onion Boy was haunted by the shadow.

Tyler took a deep breath, sitting up to face his friend. "We can't just sit here and wait, can we?"

Onion Boy's colours shifted to a resigned green, his head dipping slightly as though in agreement.

"We need to figure out what this thing is," Tyler continued, feeling a surge of determination. "Maybe it's after you, but you don't have to face it alone. If it's in this world, maybe… maybe I can help."

Onion Boy's gaze lifted, and his glow brightened slightly, flickering with a hopeful blue. Tyler could see the gratitude in his friend's eyes, but there was also a touch of worry. He knew that facing the shadow wouldn't be easy.

Tyler lay back, his mind racing with plans and questions. If the shadow was after Onion Boy, they needed to find a way to keep him safe. But where could they even start? It wasn't as if they could just walk up to the shadow and ask it to leave.

The next morning, Tyler couldn't hold back his curiosity. He waited for Mary after class, his heart pounding as he wondered if he could trust her with more information. She was observant, resourceful—and she'd been loyal enough to keep Onion Boy's secret.

"Hey, Mary," he said, catching up with her in the hallway. "Can I talk to you about something… important?"

Mary looked at him, her eyebrows arching in surprise. "Of course. Is it about Onion Boy?"

Tyler nodded, lowering his voice as he led her to a quiet spot near the school's back entrance. "There's… something else. Something I didn't tell you."

Mary listened intently as Tyler described the shadow that had appeared in his room, its twisted, shifting form and the feeling of dread that followed it. He explained how Onion Boy had protected him, and how the shadow seemed to be something from Onion Boy's world.

Mary's eyes widened as she listened, her expression a mix of fascination and fear. "Do you think… it's trying to hurt Onion Boy?"

Tyler nodded slowly. "I think so. And if it's after him, I'm worried it'll keep coming back."

Mary chewed her lip, her gaze thoughtful. "Then we need to find a way to stop it."

Tyler blinked, surprised at her decisiveness. "You really want to help?"

"Of course I do," she replied, her voice steady. "Onion Boy is important to you, Tyler. And if he's in danger, that means you're in danger too."

A strange warmth filled Tyler's chest at her words. For once, he felt as though he wasn't alone in dealing with this impossible secret. He had someone else on his side.

"Alright," he said, nodding. "But where do we start?"

Mary thought for a moment, her gaze distant. "Maybe we could start by learning more about the shadows. If Onion Boy is from another world, there must be rules… ways to protect him."

Tyler considered this. "But how would we find out? It's not like there's a book on this stuff."

Mary smirked. "Maybe there is. We could go to the library, do some research. Or maybe we can find clues… things that might give us answers."

Tyler wasn't sure how much they could find in a library, but the idea of searching together gave him a spark of hope. They agreed to meet after school the next day to dive into whatever information they could uncover.

That night, Tyler told Onion Boy about their plan. The creature's colours flickered between yellow and blue, a mix of hope and worry. Tyler reached out, giving his friend a reassuring nod.

"We'll figure this out," he promised. "We'll find a way to keep you safe."

Onion Boy's glow softened to a warm yellow, and he floated closer, his silent presence a comforting reminder that no matter what happened, they'd face it together.

As Tyler lay back, a new sense of resolve filled him. This was no longer just a game of hiding Onion Boy. It was a fight to protect him—and Tyler was ready to do whatever it took.

A Night in the Park

The next afternoon, Tyler and Mary met outside the school library, eager to begin their search for clues about Onion Boy's world. They spent hours flipping through dusty books, browsing online articles, and whispering to each other about strange folklore and mysterious creatures. But despite their efforts, they found little that matched the description of the shadow or Onion Boy's glowing, floating form.

Tyler's spirits dipped as the sky outside darkened. He'd hoped they might stumble upon something—some story or myth that would explain what the shadow was or how to stop it. But as the last pages were turned, they realised their search had been fruitless.

Mary looked up from her book, sighing. "Maybe we're looking in the wrong place."

"Maybe," Tyler agreed, closing his book with a heavy thud. "But where else can we look?"

Mary leaned forward, her eyes sparkling with a sudden idea. "What if we went to the park tonight? It's quiet, there are fewer lights, and… well, maybe Onion Boy could show us more of his world. If he's comfortable, that is."

Tyler hesitated. The idea of being out in the dark, especially with the shadow lurking somewhere, made his skin prickle. But he knew Mary had a point. Onion Boy might be able to reveal something he couldn't show indoors.

"Alright," he said, steeling himself. "We'll go after dark."

That evening, Tyler waited until his parents were settled before slipping out of the house. He met Mary near the entrance of the park, the faint glow of Onion Boy trailing behind him. Mary gave Onion Boy a small wave as he floated between them, his colours a soft blue, flickering with hints of nervous green.

The park was eerily quiet, the usual buzz of insects replaced by a heavy, unsettling silence. The moon cast pale beams of light across the empty benches and winding paths, giving everything a ghostly glow. Tyler felt a chill run down his spine as they ventured deeper into the park, Onion Boy hovering close to his shoulder.

"Alright, Onion Boy," Tyler whispered, his voice barely above a breath. "Can you… show us more of your world?"

Onion Boy's glow intensified, shifting to a warm yellow. He drifted forward, casting a soft light that painted strange, shifting images onto the trees around them. Tyler and Mary watched in awe as scenes from Onion Boy's world emerged in the darkness: glowing forests, towering plants with shimmering leaves, and other floating beings like Onion Boy, each radiating colours more vivid than anything they'd seen before.

"It's beautiful," Mary murmured, her voice filled with wonder.

But then, the images grew darker. Onion Boy's colours shifted to a deep, anxious green as the familiar shadow appeared on the trees, lurking among the vibrant shapes. Tyler could feel the shadow's presence, cold and menacing, as it loomed closer in the projection.

"What is it?" Tyler whispered. "Is it following you?"

Onion Boy's glow turned a deep blue, almost mournful. He seemed to be trying to communicate something important, something beyond simple words. Tyler strained to understand, feeling the weight of Onion Boy's sadness.

But before he could ask anything more, a rustling sound broke through the quiet.

Tyler and Mary spun around, their hearts pounding as they scanned the darkness. The sound grew louder, and suddenly, a figure emerged from the shadows—a figure draped in a long, dark coat, its face hidden beneath the brim of a wide hat.

The figure stopped a few feet away, and Tyler could feel his pulse hammering in his ears. Mary took a step closer to him, her hand gripping his arm tightly.

"Who… who are you?" Tyler stammered, his voice barely steady.

The figure tilted its head, a faint chuckle escaping from the shadows. "I see you've found yourself a friend from another world," the figure murmured, his voice low and smooth, sending a chill down Tyler's spine.

Tyler's grip tightened on Onion Boy, who floated defensively between them, his glow shifting to a protective red.

The figure took a step forward, his presence filling the air with a suffocating darkness. "The little creature doesn't belong here, you know," he continued, his tone almost taunting. "He's drawn something dangerous into your world. Something that will come for him… and anyone who tries to protect him."

Tyler swallowed, his voice shaking. "Who are you? And what… what do you want?"

The figure chuckled again, the sound echoing through the empty park. "I'm simply a messenger. But heed my warning: that shadow is relentless. It will find him, and it will not stop until he's returned to where he came from."

The figure leaned closer, his voice lowering to a whisper. “Are you willing to risk your safety… for a creature you barely know?”

Tyler met the figure’s hidden gaze, feeling a surge of protectiveness rise within him. “Yes. I don’t care what it takes. I won’t let anything happen to him.”

The figure seemed to pause, his head tilting slightly as if surprised by Tyler’s response. After a moment, he straightened, his dark silhouette fading slightly into the shadows. “Very well,” he said softly. “But remember, boy… the shadow will come.”

With those final words, the figure stepped back, melting into the darkness as quickly as he’d appeared. The silence returned, heavier than before, and Tyler let out a shaky breath, glancing at Mary, who looked equally shaken.

Onion Boy hovered close to him, his colours a muted blue, flickering with traces of fear.

“We need to get home,” Mary whispered, her voice trembling. “And… we need to figure out what we’re going to do.”

Tyler nodded, his determination hardening. The mysterious figure’s warning only strengthened his resolve. He didn’t care what dangers lay ahead—he’d do whatever it took to protect Onion Boy.

As they left the park, Onion Boy faded from sight, but Tyler could still feel his presence—a silent promise in the darkness. They were bound together now, more than ever, and Tyler knew that whatever came next, they'd face it as friends.

The Warning Comes True

The night after their encounter with the mysterious figure in the park, Tyler lay wide awake, the warning echoing in his mind: *The shadow will come.*

He tried to shake it off, to convince himself that it was just a trick of his imagination. But as the house settled into silence and shadows crept along his walls, he couldn't ignore the feeling of dread.

Suddenly, he heard a soft hiss beside him. He turned to see Onion Boy hovering close, his colours dim, flickering between dark greens and greys. Tyler's heart sank. Onion Boy was afraid too.

"It's alright," Tyler whispered, trying to sound braver than he felt. "We'll get through this."

Just as he spoke, a cold draft swept through the room, chilling him to the bone. The air grew heavy, and the shadows seemed to thicken, moving almost as if they were alive. Tyler's pulse quickened, and Onion Boy's colours shifted to a defensive red, floating protectively beside him.

Then, in the far corner of the room, the darkness began to move, slowly coalescing into the shape of a tall, twisted shadow.

Tyler gasped, instinctively grabbing his torch from his bedside table. He turned it on, shining the beam directly at the shadow, hoping the light would make it vanish. But the shadow only shifted, twisting and bending, barely affected by the light.

Onion Boy hissed again, his colours flaring brightly as he projected an image onto the wall: a strange, circular symbol, one Tyler had never seen before.

Tyler's eyes widened as he realised Onion Boy was trying to show him something important. "Is this… something that can protect us?"

The shadow seemed to grow larger, inching closer as Tyler tried to memorise the symbol's intricate design. Then, just as the shadow moved within reach, Onion Boy surged forward, his glow blazing in a bright, protective red that made the shadow recoil momentarily.

Tyler grabbed his phone, quickly snapping a picture of the symbol. "We'll find a way to stop it, Onion Boy," he promised, his voice trembling. "We'll figure out what that symbol means."

The shadow lingered for a moment longer, then melted back into the darkness, leaving only the memory of its icy presence.

Tyler took a shaky breath, looking at Onion Boy, whose colours had softened to a relieved blue. They had narrowly escaped this time, but Tyler knew they couldn't keep relying on luck. They needed real answers.

Uncle Hargreaves' Secrets

The next morning, Tyler barely waited for school to end before rushing to find Mary. He showed her the picture of the symbol and told her about the shadow's latest attack. Mary's face grew pale as she listened, but her eyes sparked with determination.

"We need help, Tyler. Real help," she said. "Doesn't your Uncle Hargreaves know about… weird things like this?"

Tyler nodded slowly. Uncle Hargreaves was the family's eccentric, known for his cluttered house filled with books and strange artifacts. He rarely spoke about what he did, but Tyler remembered stories of Uncle Hargreaves studying myths, symbols, and legends from around the world.

That afternoon, Tyler and Mary made their way to Uncle Hargreaves' house, Onion Boy floating invisibly beside them. When they arrived, Tyler took a deep breath, bracing himself as he knocked on the door. A moment later, the door creaked open, and Uncle Hargreaves appeared, his eyes bright with curiosity as he took in the sight of his nephew and Mary.

“Ah, Tyler! And a friend, I see. What brings you two to my little cave of wonders?” he asked with a small smile, stepping aside to let them in.

Tyler glanced at Mary before speaking. “Uncle Hargreaves, we need your help. We’ve… come across something strange, and we’re hoping you might know what it is.”

Hargreaves’ eyebrows rose as he led them to his study, a room filled with shelves upon shelves of books, jars of oddities, and ancient-looking relics. He settled into an old armchair, gesturing for Tyler and Mary to sit.

“Go on, then,” he said, his gaze sharp and intrigued.

Tyler showed him the picture of the symbol on his phone, explaining how Onion Boy had projected it onto the wall during the shadow’s attack. As he spoke, Onion Boy appeared beside him, his glow shifting to a cautious yellow. Uncle Hargreaves’ eyes widened at the sight of Onion Boy, but he listened without interrupting.

When Tyler finished, Hargreaves leaned forward, studying the symbol closely. “This is… an ancient symbol, Tyler. One not many would recognise. It’s associated with an old order known as the Shadow Hunters.”

Tyler exchanged a look with Mary, both of them holding their breath as Uncle Hargreaves continued.

“Shadow Hunters are rare,” he said, his tone grave. “They were individuals with a unique bond to creatures from other worlds. Beings like your friend here,” he added, nodding toward Onion Boy. “The bond gives them the ability to protect against shadow entities, creatures that slip between worlds and feed on energy.”

“Does that mean… I’m supposed to be a Shadow Hunter?” Tyler asked, his voice barely above a whisper.

Uncle Hargreaves nodded thoughtfully. “It’s possible. When such a creature bonds with a human, it often means the person has a unique role to play—a purpose that only they can fulfil. Your connection to Onion Boy may have awakened the shadow’s interest, drawing it here.”

Mary frowned. “So, the shadow wants Onion Boy… but why?”

Hargreaves leaned back, his gaze distant. “Shadows are drawn to the light of creatures from other realms. They consume that light, gaining power. But if they take too much, the creature’s essence fades, and it can never return to its world.”

Tyler’s heart clenched. He glanced at Onion Boy, whose colours had dimmed to a frightened shade of green.

"What about the symbol?" Tyler asked. "Can it protect us?"

Hargreaves nodded, getting up and rummaging through a nearby shelf. He returned with a dusty book, flipping through its pages until he found the same symbol. "This is a warding symbol. It's been used for centuries to repel shadows. Draw it in places you need to protect—your home, the doors, the windows. Shadows cannot easily cross it."

Tyler took a deep breath, a spark of hope igniting in his chest. "So, if we use this, we can keep the shadow away from Onion Boy?"

"Temporarily," Hargreaves said. "But shadows are persistent. It may weaken them, but it won't stop them forever. Shadows are clever, and they find ways around wards if given enough time."

Tyler nodded, feeling the weight of responsibility settle over him. "Thank you, Uncle Hargreaves. We'll do everything we can."

As they prepared to leave, Hargreaves placed a hand on Tyler's shoulder. "Remember, Tyler, this is no small task. Being connected to a creature like Onion Boy is a rare gift, but it comes with dangers. If you're to face this shadow, you'll need courage, trust, and above all, unity."

Tyler nodded, his gaze steady. "I understand. And I won't let anything happen to him."

Onion Boy's colours brightened to a warm yellow, his glow radiating a sense of gratitude and relief. As they left Hargreaves' house, Tyler felt a renewed sense of determination. They had a way to protect Onion Boy, at least for now. But he knew that a greater challenge lay ahead—a battle that would test everything he'd come to believe about friendship, bravery, and the unknown.

The Power Within

Since their visit to Uncle Hargreaves, Tyler couldn't shake the feeling that something had changed. Knowing he might be connected to the ancient order of Shadow Hunters made him see himself differently. And as he spent more time with Onion Boy, he began to feel strange sensations—tingling energy, warmth, and sometimes a flicker of something stronger.

One evening, while practising the warding symbol at home, Tyler held a pen in his hand, carefully tracing the lines as Uncle Hargreaves had shown him. As he focused, he felt a soft pulse, like a current running from his fingers to the paper. Suddenly, the lines on the paper started to glow faintly, casting a soft light that surprised him.

Tyler jerked his hand back, staring at the symbol. *Did I... do that?*

Onion Boy hovered close, his colours shifting to an encouraging yellow. Tyler realised Onion Boy had sensed the change too, and his friend looked proud.

"Is this… part of being a Shadow Hunter?" Tyler wondered aloud, feeling a surge of excitement.

The next day, he told Mary about what had happened, and her eyes lit up with excitement. "That's amazing, Tyler! If you're developing powers, maybe you could use them to defend against the shadow!"

Tyler nodded, feeling a growing sense of responsibility. He wasn't sure if he was ready, but he knew he had to try.

That evening, they met in the park to practise, with Onion Boy helping Tyler explore his newfound abilities. At Mary's suggestion, Onion Boy projected smaller, harmless shadows onto the wall for Tyler to confront. Tyler focused, drawing on the energy within him, and found that he could strengthen the light from his torch, making it brighter and more powerful with his intent.

After several attempts, Tyler managed to repel even the strongest of Onion Boy's projections, feeling his confidence grow with each success.

By the end of the evening, Tyler felt exhausted but accomplished. For the first time, he believed he might truly be able to protect Onion Boy from the looming shadow. As they walked home, he held Onion Boy's gaze, silently promising that he would keep him safe, no matter the cost.

The Shadow’s Warning

The following night, Tyler was alone in his room, the usual quiet settling over him as he prepared to sleep. Onion Boy had already faded out, but Tyler could still feel his comforting presence nearby. He lay back, trying to relax, when an unnatural chill swept through the room.

Suddenly, the shadows on his wall began to twist, gathering into a single, defined shape. Tyler froze, his heart racing as he realised the shadow was no longer hiding in corners—it was standing boldly before him, taller and darker than ever.

The shadow’s form shifted, becoming more menacing, with a set of faint, glowing eyes that locked onto Tyler. For the first time, the shadow’s presence felt overpowering, filling the room with a sense of dread.

Then, in a low, rasping voice, it spoke: “Your bond with that creature is a mistake.”

Tyler swallowed, his heart hammering in his chest, but he refused to back down. “Leave us alone!” he demanded, his voice steadier than he felt.

The shadow chuckled, a dark, hollow sound that echoed around him. “You cannot protect it. The creature’s light is unnatural in this world. It doesn’t belong here, and neither do you.”

Tyler clenched his fists, anger and fear mixing within him. “I don’t care what you say. I won’t let you hurt him.”

The shadow’s eyes narrowed, and its voice dropped to a chilling whisper. “Then you shall suffer for this defiance. Your connection to the creature endangers you, your family, everyone you care about. Sever the bond, or pay the price.”

As the shadow moved closer, Tyler felt an instinctive surge of energy rise within him. Without thinking, he reached for the symbol he’d drawn earlier, holding it up with determination. To his surprise, he felt warmth radiate from his hand, amplifying the light of the symbol and casting a bright glow across the room.

Onion Boy appeared beside him, his colours blazing in a powerful red, joining Tyler’s energy to drive the shadow back. The combined force of Tyler’s light and Onion Boy’s glow pushed the shadow to the edges of the room. With a final, furious hiss, it melted into the darkness, retreating but not disappearing entirely.

Tyler sat back, breathless but resolute. He had confronted the shadow and, with Onion Boy's help, forced it to back down. But he knew this was far from over—the shadow would return, angrier and stronger.

The next day, Tyler told Mary everything, his voice filled with a new resolve. "The shadow's not going to stop. It's going to keep coming after Onion Boy and anyone close to him."

Mary nodded, her face pale but determined. "Then we have to be ready. We'll keep practising, keep learning, until we're strong enough to face it head-on."

As they prepared for what lay ahead, Tyler felt a powerful sense of purpose. He was no longer just a boy with a strange friend; he was a protector, and he would face whatever dangers came his way to keep Onion Boy safe.

Practicing the Light

The next few days passed in a blur of training, and Tyler barely had a moment to breathe. He and Mary spent every spare minute practising in the park, pushing the limits of what Tyler could do. With Onion Boy's help, they worked on using light and warding symbols to defend against small, harmless shadow projections that Onion Boy created.

One afternoon, after school, Tyler held a piece of chalk in his hand, tracing the warding symbol onto the ground as Mary watched. When he finished, he placed his palm over it, focusing his energy the way Uncle Hargreaves had taught him.

"Come on, Tyler," Mary encouraged, her eyes bright with excitement. "Focus on everything Onion Boy means to you."

Tyler took a deep breath, channelling all his emotions—the loyalty, the protectiveness, and the friendship he felt for Onion Boy. Slowly, he felt a warmth building within him, surging down his arm and into his hand. The symbol beneath his palm began to glow faintly, casting a soft, comforting light over the ground.

Mary gasped, her eyes wide. "You did it! It's working!"

Tyler grinned, feeling a rush of pride. But just as the symbol's light grew stronger, he felt the familiar, chilling sensation of darkness pressing in. Onion Boy appeared beside him, his colours flickering nervously between shades of green and blue. Without warning, he projected a series of images onto the wall of the park's shed.

Tyler and Mary turned to watch as scenes from Onion Boy's world unfolded before them. There were forests filled with glowing lights, fields of strange, otherworldly plants, and creatures similar to Onion Boy. But then the image darkened, and a figure appeared—an enormous shadow, twisting and contorting as it moved through Onion Boy's world, devouring everything in its path.

Tyler's chest tightened as he realised what Onion Boy was showing them. "This shadow… it's been hunting you, hasn't it?"

Onion Boy's colours shifted to a sorrowful shade of grey, and he nodded slowly.

Mary frowned, her gaze dark. "So this shadow is some kind of… predator. It's after Onion Boy's light."

Tyler felt a surge of protectiveness, clenching his fists as he faced the images on the wall. “Then we’ll stop it. We’ll protect you, Onion Boy.”

Onion Boy’s colours softened to a grateful yellow, his glow wrapping around Tyler and Mary like a comforting blanket. Tyler placed his hand back over the glowing symbol, feeling a renewed sense of purpose. Whatever it took, he would protect his friend.

With that, Tyler redoubled his efforts, practising the warding symbols, amplifying his light, and finding strength he hadn’t known he had. By the time they left the park, Tyler was exhausted, but he felt stronger, more prepared for the battle that lay ahead.

The First Real Battle

That night, Tyler settled into bed, his body aching from the day's training. He lay back, closing his eyes, hoping for a peaceful night's sleep. But as the room darkened and silence filled the house, a chill swept through the air, sending a shiver down his spine.

He opened his eyes, feeling the familiar presence of something sinister. His room felt heavier, as if an unseen weight were pressing down on him. And then, he saw it.

In the far corner of his room, the shadow emerged, larger and more defined than ever. Its twisted form shifted and swayed, and Tyler felt a wave of terror wash over him as he realised the shadow wasn't here to threaten—it was here to take.

Onion Boy appeared beside him, his colours blazing in a fierce red as he floated between Tyler and the shadow. Tyler grabbed the piece of chalk from his bedside table, quickly drawing the warding symbol on the floor, his hands trembling as he struggled to focus.

The shadow lunged, moving faster than Tyler had ever seen. It swept across the room like a dark cloud, aiming straight for Onion Boy. Tyler barely had time to react, his heart pounding as he threw himself in front of his friend, holding his hands out defensively.

To his surprise, he felt a surge of warmth within him, and his hands began to glow with a soft, radiant light. The shadow recoiled slightly, momentarily halted by the intensity of the glow. Tyler took a deep breath, focusing on the bond he shared with Onion Boy, feeling the warmth spread through his chest.

"Leave us alone!" he shouted, his voice filled with determination.

The shadow paused, almost as if it were taken aback, but then it lunged forward again, its twisted form filling the room with an oppressive darkness. Tyler stumbled back, his hand brushing the warding symbol on the floor. The symbol pulsed with light, and Tyler felt the warmth intensify, amplifying his energy.

With renewed strength, Tyler placed his hand over the symbol, pouring his emotions into it. The symbol glowed brighter, casting a fierce light that pushed the shadow back.

Onion Boy's colours flared in solidarity, his glow merging with Tyler's light to create a shield that held the shadow at bay.

But the shadow was relentless. It pressed against the shield, its form distorting as it tried to break through. Tyler felt his strength waning, the energy draining from him as he struggled to maintain the shield.

In a final, desperate move, Tyler focused on everything he loved about Onion Boy—the laughter, the companionship, the loyalty. A surge of light erupted from his hands, forcing the shadow back with a hiss. The dark figure retreated to the corner, melting into the darkness and leaving only a lingering chill.

Tyler collapsed onto his bed, his body heavy with exhaustion. He'd managed to repel the shadow, but he knew it was only a temporary victory. The shadow would return, and next time, it would be even stronger.

The next morning, Tyler confided in Mary, his voice trembling with a mixture of fear and determination. "The shadow's not going to stop, Mary. It's coming for Onion Boy… and for anyone close to him."

Mary's eyes were wide, but her jaw was set. "Then we'll be ready. We'll keep practising, keep fighting, until we're strong enough to end this for good."

Together, they walked to the park to continue their training, knowing that the battle was far from over. But Tyler felt a new resolve growing within him. He would protect Onion Boy, no matter the cost. And with Mary by his side, he knew they stood a fighting chance.

A Search for Answers

After the most recent encounter with the shadow, Tyler's fear lingered, pressing on him even in daylight. He and Mary knew that to protect Onion Boy and themselves, they'd need more than just the symbols they had been using. With no time to waste, they headed back to Uncle Hargreaves, hoping he could help them find something stronger.

When they arrived, Uncle Hargreaves was deep in a pile of dusty old books, surrounded by ancient maps and scrolls. He looked up, his eyes bright with curiosity. "Back for more, eh?" he said, studying their worried faces. "You've stirred up something powerful, haven't you?"

Tyler nodded. "The shadow isn't going to stop, Uncle. We need something… more powerful. Is there anything else you can teach us?"

Hargreaves pondered for a moment, flipping through a thick, leather-bound book before looking at them with a serious expression. “There’s mention of creatures like your friend Onion Boy—beings of light who’ve crossed into our world. But wherever there’s light, darkness follows. Shadows have hunted beings like him for centuries.”

He pulled out an old, fragile book and turned to a page depicting a familiar symbol, surrounded by strange markings and symbols. “This is part of an ancient text called the **Book of Shadows**,” he explained. “It’s a rare book with secrets about warding off shadow entities. If you can find it, it may hold the key to permanently protecting your friend.”

Tyler and Mary shared a look, their excitement mixed with a sense of urgency. “Where can we find it?” Mary asked.

Hargreaves rubbed his chin thoughtfully. “It’s likely in the town’s oldest library. Or, perhaps… hidden right here.” He gestured to the piles of books surrounding them, chuckling softly. “This place is practically a library itself.”

Not wanting to waste a second, Tyler and Mary set to work, carefully combing through stacks of books, hunting for any sign of the **Book of Shadows**. As they searched, Onion Boy floated quietly beside them, his colours a calming shade of blue, sensing their determination.

Hours passed, but just as their hope was beginning to fade, Mary let out a small gasp. “Tyler! Look!”

She pulled a dark, ancient-looking book from a stack in the corner, its cover embossed with a faint image of the symbol they'd been practising. She carefully opened it to reveal pages filled with detailed drawings of shadows, warding symbols, and ancient creatures of light.

Uncle Hargreaves looked over her shoulder, nodding approvingly. "The **Book of Shadows**," he murmured. "You're on the right path, Tyler."

Tyler's heart raced as he flipped through the book, each page revealing new secrets and rituals. His fingers trembled as he scanned passages about warding symbols, protective spells, and—on a single page near the end—a mention of a powerful item known as the **Light Stone**.

"This… this could be it," Tyler whispered, glancing at Onion Boy, who was glowing a curious shade of yellow.

The Secret Weapon

Tyler, Mary, and Onion Boy gathered at Uncle Hargreaves' house the following day, eager to dive deeper into the Book of Shadows. As they read, they discovered that the Light Stone was an ancient crystal, rumoured to hold enough light energy to repel shadows permanently.

"If we find this stone, it might be the key to keeping Onion Boy safe for good," Tyler said, his voice filled with determination.

Uncle Hargreaves pointed to an illustration of the Light Stone, its facets radiating with beams of light. "It's not just any crystal," he explained. "The Light Stone amplifies the powers of those connected to creatures of light. In the hands of someone with a bond like yours, Tyler, it could unleash immense protective energy."

As Tyler studied the page, he realised they'd need to perform a ritual to activate the stone. The instructions were complex, involving symbols and chants from the Book of Shadows, which Hargreaves translated for them with care. Tyler took detailed notes, feeling the weight of the task ahead but also the hope that they'd finally found a way to protect Onion Boy.

But finding the Light Stone would be a challenge. The Book of Shadows hinted that it was hidden away in an ancient place of power, likely near the edge of town where few dared to go. Mary's eyes sparkled with a mix of fear and excitement. "So, we have to go on a bit of an adventure," she said, trying to sound braver than she felt.

Tyler nodded, his gaze steely. "This is the only way to stop the shadow."

That evening, they prepared for the journey. Mary brought her torch, some chalk, and a small knife in case they needed to etch symbols along the way. Tyler studied the map Hargreaves had given them, memorising the path to where the Light Stone might be hidden.

As the sun set, Onion Boy hovered beside them, his colours brightening and shifting to deep, determined hues of purple and blue. Tyler could feel Onion Boy's energy strengthening, as if the mention of the Light Stone had unlocked something within him.

As they practised the new rituals, Onion Boy began to show an incredible ability. He created a glowing shield around Tyler, a barrier of light that shimmered in a spectrum of colours. Tyler felt protected, as if nothing could harm him while Onion Boy's glow surrounded him.

"It's working," Mary whispered, watching Onion Boy in awe. "You're both becoming stronger."

Tyler smiled, feeling a surge of pride. They were closer than ever to protecting Onion Boy—and maybe even defeating the shadow once and for all. They spent the next hours going over every detail of the journey, feeling both nervous and prepared for the challenges ahead.

As they walked home that night, Tyler felt a renewed sense of purpose. The shadow was growing stronger, but with the Book of Shadows, Onion Boy's evolving powers, and the hope of finding the Light Stone, they stood a real chance.

They were no longer just defending against the shadow—they were ready to fight back.

The Journey to the Stone

Tyler's heart raced as he, Mary, and Onion Bovy set out on their journey. The map from Uncle Hargreaves guided them through a path barely visible in the evening light, leading them toward the edge of town, where tall, twisted trees created an ominous canopy overhead.

"Are you sure about this?" Mary whispered, clutching her torch tightly.

Tyler nodded, trying to appear braver than he felt. "This is the only way to keep Onion Boy safe."

Onion Boy floated close, his colours flickering between blue and green as he cast a faint, reassuring light over their path. But even his glow couldn't fully dispel the creeping shadows that seemed to follow them, shifting and bending in unnatural ways.

As they walked, strange sensations began to settle around them. They heard faint whispers on the wind, murmurs that Tyler couldn't quite understand but sent a chill down his spine. He could see the tension in Mary's face, her eyes darting around, watching every flicker in the darkness.

"I don't like this," she muttered. "It feels like… something's watching us."

Tyler swallowed, glancing over his shoulder, half-expecting the shadow to emerge. But each time he looked, there was nothing there—just an unsettling quiet.

They continued along the path, reaching a broken wooden bridge spanning a narrow but deep gorge. The old planks creaked under their weight, but they managed to cross safely, each step bringing them closer to the ancient ground they sought.

As they climbed a rocky incline, Tyler slipped, catching himself just in time. Onion Boy's glow intensified, guiding him as he scrambled up the final few feet. When he looked back, he saw Mary's hand extended, her expression a mix of worry and determination.

"Almost there," Tyler said, nodding toward a faint glow just beyond a cluster of trees.

They pushed forward, stepping into a large clearing surrounded by rocks engraved with strange, glowing symbols. Tyler felt a rush of energy the moment he entered, as though the very ground beneath his feet recognised him.

Mary took a deep breath. "This… this has to be it."

In the centre of the clearing, on a stone pedestal, lay the Light Stone—a crystal about the size of Tyler's hand, emitting a soft, warm light that made him feel safe and powerful. He reached out carefully, his fingers brushing the crystal's surface, feeling a surge of energy flow through him.

But just as he closed his fingers around the stone, a chill swept through the clearing.

Facing the Shadow's Trap

The air thickened as a dark fog crept into the clearing, snuffing out the light from the glowing symbols around them. The shadows coiled and twisted, merging into a single form that towered over them, its eyes like cold, dark flames fixed on Onion Boy.

"Tyler!" Mary shouted, holding her torch out defensively, though its beam barely penetrated the fog.

Tyler clutched the Light Stone tightly, feeling its warmth in his hand. He held it up, hoping to channel its energy. A beam of light shot from the stone, forming a shield around Onion Boy. But the shadow moved closer, swirling around them, relentless.

The shadow twisted, lashing out with tendrils of darkness that slammed against the light shield, shaking Tyler to his core. He gritted his teeth, focusing on the warmth of the Light Stone, determined to protect Onion Boy. But the shadow was powerful, its darkness pressing harder, breaking through cracks in the shield.

"Mary, the symbols!" Tyler shouted.

Mary grabbed her chalk, quickly drawing the warding symbols around the clearing, her hands trembling. Each symbol emitted a faint light, but it wasn't enough to keep the shadow at bay. It pushed forward, its dark form expanding, absorbing the light.

Tyler felt his energy draining as he struggled to hold the shield, his mind racing. The Light Stone alone wasn't strong enough—they needed more power, something that would turn the tide.

Onion Boy, sensing Tyler's desperation, floated forward, his colours shifting to a fierce, determined red. He focused his light, directing it toward the shadow with a force Tyler hadn't seen before. Together, their combined light managed to force the shadow back a few feet, but it was only a momentary reprieve.

The shadow hissed, its dark form swirling in anger, and it lashed out again. This time, its attack shattered the shield, and Tyler stumbled back, his hands trembling.

"Tyler, look out!" Mary screamed.

The shadow lunged, aiming directly for Onion Boy, its tendrils of darkness wrapping around him. Tyler felt a surge of panic as he watched his friend struggle against the shadow's grip, his glow flickering dangerously.

With a surge of desperation, Tyler held the Light Stone aloft, focusing every ounce of energy he had left. "Leave us alone!" he shouted, his voice echoing through the clearing.

The stone pulsed with light, emitting a blinding glow that forced the shadow back, its form distorting as it recoiled. But even as it retreated, Tyler could feel its presence lingering, a dark promise that it would return.

The shadow finally dissolved into the night, leaving the clearing cold and silent. Tyler collapsed to his knees, his breath coming in gasps, the Light Stone still glowing faintly in his hand. Onion Boy floated beside him, his colours a pale, exhausted blue.

Mary knelt beside them, her face pale. "Are… are you alright?"

Tyler nodded weakly. "We drove it back… but it's not gone. The Light Stone helped, but… it wasn't enough."

They shared a heavy silence, the weight of their near-defeat sinking in. The shadow was stronger than they'd ever imagined, and the Light Stone alone wasn't enough to defeat it.

But as they left the clearing, a new determination took hold of Tyler. They might not have defeated the shadow this time, but they wouldn't give up. With Mary, Onion Boy, and the Book of Shadows to guide them, he knew they'd find a way to end this.

They had no choice.

A New Ally

Tyler and Mary returned to Uncle Hargreaves' house after their harrowing escape, still shaken from their encounter with the shadow. The Light Stone had helped, but they knew now that its power alone wasn't enough to defeat the shadow permanently.

"Uncle Hargreaves," Tyler said, his voice laced with urgency, "isn't there anyone else who knows about these shadows? There has to be someone who can help us."

Uncle Hargreaves glanced thoughtfully at Onion Boy, who hovered close, his colours a faint shade of yellow. "There is one person," Hargreaves said slowly. "In a small village not far from here lives a guardian. She's known for her knowledge of dark forces—and of light, too."

Tyler and Mary exchanged a hopeful look. "Can we meet her?" Mary asked eagerly.

With Hargreaves' directions in hand, Tyler and Mary set out with Onion Boy the next morning. The journey led them to a quiet village nestled between hills and dense forest. Following the locals' directions, they finally found themselves in front of a small, ivy-covered cottage at the edge of the village. Tyler knocked, his heart pounding with both excitement and fear.

The door creaked open, and a woman with silver hair and piercing green eyes looked them over. She was older, with a quiet strength about her, and something in her gaze suggested she understood things beyond what ordinary people could.

"You've brought a Light Keeper to me," she said softly, her eyes lingering on Onion Boy. "It's been many years since I've seen one."

The woman, who introduced herself as **Evelyn**, invited them in and listened intently as they told her about their encounters with the shadow. Her gaze softened as she heard the tale, and she nodded, as if she knew more than she was saying.

Evelyn explained, "Creatures like your friend here, Light Keepers, are rare beings. They draw strength from the light and repel darkness. But shadows are drawn to them because consuming a Light Keeper's energy grants a shadow immense power."

Tyler felt a surge of anger and protectiveness. "So this shadow… it wants Onion Boy's energy?"

"Yes," Evelyn replied, her voice serious. "But it's more than that. Shadows hunt beings of light not just for their energy, but because it gives them purpose. The shadow that follows you has grown powerful because of your connection to the Light Keeper."

Evelyn led them to a shelf, pulling down an ancient, worn box. Inside, nestled on a bed of silk, was a pendant with a small, glowing crystal—the **Light Amulet**.

"This amulet will enhance your bond with Onion Boy," Evelyn explained. "It draws out the energy in your connection, strengthening both of you. But remember, to use it effectively, you must be fearless, and you must trust each other completely. Only then will it unlock its true power."

Tyler felt the weight of her words. He'd trusted Onion Boy with his life, but this amulet would test that trust in new ways. He exchanged a determined look with Mary, who nodded in encouragement.

Taking the amulet, Tyler thanked Evelyn, feeling a renewed sense of purpose. As they left, Evelyn called after them, "Be careful, Tyler. Shadows are clever, and they will use your doubts against you. Hold fast to the light, even in the darkest moments."

The Shadow's True Power

With the Light Amulet in hand, Tyler, Mary, and Onion Boy returned home, determined to test the amulet's abilities. Tyler wore it around his neck, feeling a faint warmth radiating from it, amplifying his connection with Onion Boy.

As night fell, Tyler felt more confident than ever. But just as he was settling down, a familiar, icy presence filled the room. The shadow had returned, stronger, darker, and more terrifying than before.

Mary, who had stayed to support Tyler, turned on her torch, casting a bright beam across the room. But the shadow didn't recoil as it had before. Instead, it seemed to absorb the light, growing even darker and more solid as it spread across the walls.

"What's it doing?" Mary whispered, fear creeping into her voice.

Tyler gripped the amulet, focusing on the warmth of his bond with Onion Boy. He channelled his energy, creating a bright shield of light around Onion Boy, but the shadow pressed forward, unaffected.

Then, a deep, rumbling voice filled the room, echoing with dark, twisted power. “You think a mere pendant can save you?”

Tyler’s heart pounded as he watched the shadow, its form solidifying, taking on a human-like shape. Its eyes were dark, hollow, and its voice was filled with anger and bitterness. “I was once like your friend,” it said, its tone laced with resentment. “A creature of light, bound to a human. But when they abandoned me, I turned to the darkness.”

Tyler’s hand trembled as he absorbed the revelation. This shadow, once a creature like Onion Boy, had been abandoned and transformed by anger, left alone to fester in darkness until it became something twisted and hateful.

“Is that why you’re hunting Onion Boy?” Tyler demanded. “Because you think we’ll abandon him?”

The shadow’s form shifted, becoming more menacing. “You will abandon him. All humans do. And when you do, I will be waiting.”

Tyler felt a flicker of doubt. He’d promised to protect Onion Boy, but could he really be there forever? His heart raced, and the shadow seemed to grow stronger, feeding off his uncertainty.

"Tyler, don't listen to it!" Mary cried, grabbing his arm. "The shadow is trying to make you doubt yourself. That's how it gains power."

Tyler looked down at Onion Boy, whose colours flickered a determined red. Taking a deep breath, he refocused, pushing away his doubts and trusting fully in his bond with Onion Boy. He channelled his energy through the Light Amulet, creating a powerful, radiant light that cut through the shadow's darkness.

The shadow hissed, recoiling slightly, but it didn't retreat. It pushed back, its form stretching and twisting, filling the room with a darkness so thick it felt suffocating.

"Tyler, the amulet!" Mary urged. "Trust in your connection with Onion Boy!"

Tyler closed his eyes, reaching out to Onion Boy with his heart and mind, drawing strength from their friendship. He felt a surge of warmth flood through him, igniting the amulet with a blinding light. The energy enveloped Onion Boy, intensifying his glow until the room was filled with radiant colours.

For a brief moment, the shadow seemed to falter, its form flickering as though weakened. But just as they thought they'd gained the upper hand, it let out a chilling laugh, reforming stronger than ever.

"You cannot defeat me with light alone," it sneered. "The darkness is in your heart as well. Until you face that, I will always return."

The shadow melted into the darkness, leaving Tyler shaken and exhausted, clutching the amulet. He exchanged a troubled look with Mary, realising the truth: the shadow wasn't just an enemy to be fought—it was a reflection of fear, doubt, and darkness within.

As they gathered their thoughts, Tyler understood what Evelyn meant: defeating the shadow would require more than strength and light. He'd have to confront the darkness within himself as well.

Together, Tyler, Mary, and Onion Boy knew they'd need more than just courage to face what lay ahead. They'd need to dig deep, face their fears, and strengthen the bond they shared if they were to stand a chance against the shadow once and for all.

Confronting Inner Fears

Tyler sat alone in his room, the shadow's words echoing in his mind: *The darkness is in your heart as well.* It was a haunting statement, one that burrowed deep into his thoughts, and he found himself questioning whether he was truly strong enough to protect Onion Boy.

The following morning, he confided in Mary as they walked through the park. "What if the shadow's right?" he asked quietly. "What if I'm not strong enough? What if I let Onion Boy down?"

Mary stopped, placing a hand on his shoulder. "Tyler, you're the bravest person I know. You haven't let Onion Boy down once. But maybe… maybe the shadow's feeding on your doubts. If we face what's inside, maybe it won't have power over you anymore."

Tyler nodded, taking a deep breath. He felt the weight of his insecurities pressing down, but Mary's words gave him hope. Together, they retraced the places where Tyler's self-doubt had first taken root—the schoolyard where he'd once felt small, his family home where he'd sometimes felt overlooked, and even the empty spaces in the park where he'd hidden from bullies.

As they walked, Onion Boy floated close, his warm yellow glow flickering like a reassuring hand on Tyler's shoulder. Tyler felt the bond between them deepen, a quiet but powerful strength growing in his heart. It was as though Onion Boy could feel every struggle and triumph, sharing the experience alongside him.

Later that evening, Tyler sat alone in his room, reflecting on the journey he'd taken. He realised that while his fears were real, they didn't define him. With Onion Boy and Mary by his side, he felt braver, more prepared to face whatever darkness lay ahead.

When he shared his feelings with Onion Boy, the little creature glowed a brilliant shade of green and purple, his colours full of hope. Tyler sensed that their connection had strengthened beyond words; it was a silent promise of loyalty and trust.

Now, with his fears acknowledged and his heart fortified, Tyler felt ready. They would face the shadow one last time—and this time, he'd face it with the strength of his bond and the light within him.

The Final Stand

Night fell over the town, and Tyler, Mary, and Onion Boy made their way to the clearing near the park, where the air seemed to thrum with anticipation. They'd set up protective symbols and prepared their torches, ready for the final confrontation. Tyler wore the Light Amulet around his neck, feeling its comforting warmth as he focused on the strength he'd found within himself.

A sudden chill filled the air, and a dark fog crept over the clearing. The shadow emerged, larger and more powerful than ever, its tendrils of darkness stretching across the ground, swallowing the faint light around them. It seemed to pulse with anger, its form shifting and twisting in the air.

"So, you've come to face me once more," the shadow sneered, its voice a low, mocking hiss.

Tyler stood firm, feeling the Light Amulet's energy amplify his resolve. "I'm not afraid of you anymore," he said, his voice steady. "You don't control me, and you won't take Onion Boy."

The shadow laughed, a cold, hollow sound. "I feed on your fear, on your doubts. Without them, you are nothing."

Tyler held the Light Amulet, focusing on his bond with Onion Boy. He channelled the warmth and courage he'd built up, and the amulet glowed with a radiant light that formed a shield around Onion Boy and himself. Mary joined them, quickly drawing warding symbols around the clearing, their lines emitting a faint glow that helped strengthen the barrier.

Enraged, the shadow pressed forward, lashing out with dark tendrils that struck against the light shield. Tyler felt the impact reverberate through him, but he held strong, refusing to let fear creep in. Onion Boy's glow intensified, casting a warm, steady light that pulsed in rhythm with Tyler's heartbeat.

"Mary, stay close!" Tyler shouted as the shadow grew larger, its form towering over them. He could feel it probing at his mind, trying to find cracks in his confidence. Dark visions of failure flashed before him, but he fought them off, focusing instead on the friendship and loyalty he shared with Onion Boy.

But the shadow was relentless, its presence suffocating as it closed in around them. In a bold move, Tyler stepped forward, directly confronting the darkness. "You want my fear?" he challenged. "You'll get nothing from me."

The shadow paused, momentarily taken aback by his defiance, but then reformed, its shape becoming more defined, almost human-like. It lunged, its tendrils reaching for Tyler and Onion Boy, trying to force its way through the light.

In a final act of bravery, Tyler reached for Onion Boy, holding his hand over the Light Amulet. "Together, Onion Boy. Let's show it what we're made of."

Onion Boy glowed brighter than ever, his colours shifting to a brilliant array of warm yellows, purples, and blues. Tyler focused on the love and loyalty he felt, and the Light Amulet blazed with a powerful light that filled the clearing, casting out every trace of darkness.

The shadow writhed and shrieked, its form weakening as the light consumed it. Tyler, Mary, and Onion Boy poured every ounce of their strength into the amulet, their light blending into a single, blinding beam. The shadow let out a final, anguished scream before its form began to dissolve, fading into wisps of darkness that were swallowed by the light.

As the last traces of darkness vanished, the clearing fell silent. Tyler collapsed to his knees, exhausted but triumphant. He looked at Onion Boy, whose soft, relieved glow bathed the clearing in warmth. Mary knelt beside them, her eyes wide with relief and joy.

"You did it, Tyler," she whispered. "You faced it, and you won."

Tyler felt a surge of pride, a sense of peace settling over him. He had faced the darkness within himself and emerged stronger, his bond with Onion Boy unbreakable.

As they walked back home under the soft glow of the moon, Tyler realised that the shadow was gone—but the strength he'd gained, the friendship he'd forged, would stay with him forever. Together, they'd overcome the darkness, finding light even in the deepest shadows.

A New Beginning

In the days that followed their victory over the shadow, Tyler noticed the world seemed brighter. Colours appeared sharper, the sky felt higher, and he walked with a lightness he hadn't felt in years. Every morning when he woke up, he'd look around his room, half-expecting to see the shadow lurking in a corner, only to find Onion Boy floating cheerfully beside him, his warm colours casting a gentle glow over the room.

Returning to school felt surreal. For so long, he'd been haunted by his doubts, by the looming darkness that shadowed his thoughts. But now, those anxieties had been replaced by a confidence he couldn't quite explain. He greeted Mary with a huge grin each day, their whispered conversations about their adventure filling them both with pride and nostalgia.

One day after school, Mary invited Tyler and Onion Boy to her house to celebrate what she called their "grand victory over darkness." Tyler chuckled, but he felt a warm surge of pride. The three of them had indeed taken on something bigger than any of them had ever imagined—and they'd won.

Mary's house was decorated with festive streamers and balloons she'd cobbled together at the last minute, but her effort made Tyler smile. She even set up a little table on the patio, covered with snacks and drinks, and arranged a spot for Onion Boy to hover beside them, as though he were an honoured guest.

"To the bravest team I know," Mary said, holding up a cup of fizzy soda. "We faced shadows, faced our fears, and showed we're stronger than any darkness."

Tyler raised his cup, grinning. "To friendship—and to the best teammates I could have asked for."

Onion Boy floated between them, his colours a celebratory swirl of bright orange, yellow, and a soft, content blue. It was the most vivid Tyler had ever seen him, and he felt an overwhelming sense of gratitude for the strange, wonderful friend he'd made.

As they ate and laughed, Mary grew thoughtful. "Do you think… the shadow will come back? Or others like it?"

Tyler paused, looking at Onion Boy, who floated beside him in calm, reassuring hues of green and blue. He felt the warmth of the Light Amulet tucked beneath his shirt, a reminder of the journey they'd taken and the strength they'd discovered. "I don't know," he admitted, his voice steady. "But I know that, whatever comes, we'll be ready. And I'll protect Onion Boy as long as I'm here."

Mary nodded, her expression determined. "And I'll be there, too. Always."

They clinked their cups again, a silent promise sealed under the fading light of the afternoon. The friendship and bond they shared felt as solid as the earth beneath their feet, and Tyler knew he could face anything with them by his side.

A Promise Kept

As summer turned to autumn, Tyler's life settled into a comfortable rhythm. The shadow was gone, but its memory lingered, reminding him of the strength he'd found within himself and the courage he'd shared with Onion Boy and Mary. School, once a place where he'd felt invisible, now felt full of possibilities. He found himself talking more with classmates, taking part in activities, and offering a quiet, steady confidence he'd never known he had.

Onion Boy was always near him, glowing like a warm ember on even the coldest days. They'd spend quiet evenings together, sitting on Tyler's front porch as the sky shifted from bright blue to twilight. Onion Boy would often drift over the yard, his colours reflecting the soft yellows, purples, and reds of the autumn leaves. Tyler loved those moments, sitting with his friend in the quiet peace they'd fought so hard to protect.

One crisp autumn evening, Tyler sat on his porch with Onion Boy at his side. The air was filled with the scent of woodsmoke and fallen leaves, and the stars were beginning to blink into view. Tyler looked over at Onion Boy, smiling at the calm, happy colours that pulsed softly in the dimming light.

"Do you remember when we first met?" Tyler asked, his voice a soft whisper in the evening air. "I was terrified. And you—" He chuckled, recalling the chaos Onion Boy had caused in the beginning, from startling him awake to causing trouble at school. "You were this little mischievous light I didn't know what to make of."

Onion Boy's colours shifted to a playful orange and blue, a hint of his impish personality coming through. Tyler chuckled, feeling a swell of affection for his strange, wonderful friend. "You taught me a lot, you know. More than I ever thought I'd learn."

The words hung in the air between them, unspoken promises and shared memories that neither could truly express. Tyler thought about how much he'd grown, how much courage he'd found within himself—all because of Onion Boy.

As the night deepened, Mary joined them on the porch, a warm cup of cocoa in her hands. "Thought I'd stop by," she said with a grin, settling down beside Tyler. "Figured you two might be reminiscing."

Tyler smiled, feeling a comfortable warmth spread over him. They watched the stars in silence for a while, each of them lost in their own thoughts. Finally, Mary turned to Tyler, her voice thoughtful.

"What do you think is next for us?" she asked, her gaze shifting between him and Onion Boy.

Tyler considered the question, feeling the weight of the journey they'd taken settle over him like a soft blanket. "I don't know," he said honestly. "But whatever it is, I think we'll face it together. We're… kind of a team now, right?"

Mary chuckled, holding up her cocoa cup. "To the best team in the world," she said, clinking her cup against his.

As they sat together, Tyler felt a sense of peace settle over him. He knew their journey wasn't over—there would always be challenges and new adventures. But he also knew that with friends like Mary and Onion Boy, he would never face those challenges alone.

As the stars filled the sky, Tyler made a quiet promise to himself, one he felt deep in his heart. No matter what happened, he would hold on to the courage, friendship, and light he'd found. And as long as Onion Boy was with him, he would protect that light, ensuring it would never be dimmed by darkness.

The three of them stayed on the porch late into the night, laughing, reminiscing, and dreaming of the future—a future they'd face side by side, bound by a bond that would only grow stronger with time.

Epilogue: The Next Step

It had been almost a year since Tyler, Mary, and Onion Boy had banished the shadow, and life had settled into a peaceful rhythm. The three friends were closer than ever, bound by the adventure that had tested their strength and changed them all. Tyler had become more confident, Mary had grown braver, and Onion Boy's presence was a source of warmth and joy—a constant reminder of the light they'd fought so hard to protect.

On a clear spring afternoon, Tyler, Mary, and Onion Boy strolled through the park. Birds chirped in the trees, and the scent of blooming flowers filled the air. It was hard to believe that this peaceful place had once been the scene of so much fear and darkness. Yet the memory of the shadow lingered, a silent reminder that darkness was never too far away.

They made their way to the clearing where they'd once found the Light Stone. The ancient markings on the stones were now faint and worn, as if the magic had faded, but Tyler felt a sense of pride standing there. This place was part of their story—a story that had made them stronger.

"Do you ever wonder," Mary asked, breaking the quiet, "if there are more creatures like Onion Boy out there? More worlds filled with light… or shadows?"

Tyler nodded thoughtfully. "Yeah. Sometimes I feel like this was just the beginning. Like… we're meant for something more."

Onion Boy glowed a soft, reassuring yellow, drifting around them as if to show he'd be ready for any new adventure that came their way. Tyler chuckled, reaching out to touch his friend, feeling a rush of gratitude and joy.

But then, the air grew cold. Tyler felt an odd pressure, a heaviness that settled over the clearing like a dark cloud. Onion Boy's colours shifted, dimming to a wary green as he floated closer to Tyler, sensing the change.

A low, ominous voice echoed through the clearing, sending chills down their spines.

"So… you thought you'd defeated my servant?"

Tyler and Mary froze, exchanging terrified glances. From the shadows between the trees, a figure emerged—tall, cloaked, and surrounded by a dark, rippling aura. His eyes were piercing, filled with a darkness that made the shadow they'd defeated seem small in comparison.

"I am the Master," the figure intoned, his voice dripping with malice. "The one who commands the shadows. You may have destroyed one of my servants, but I have many more—and I do not take kindly to those who meddle in my affairs."

Tyler swallowed, his heart pounding. The Master's presence was overpowering, a force of pure darkness that seemed to sap the light from the clearing. He reached for the Light Amulet around his neck, feeling its familiar warmth, but it seemed to dim in the presence of the Master.

"What do you want?" Mary demanded, her voice trembling but steady.

The Master's gaze shifted to Onion Boy, who hovered protectively in front of Tyler. "I want what was taken from me. That creature's light belongs to the shadows. And I will have my revenge for your interference."

Tyler felt a surge of protectiveness. He tightened his grip on the Light Amulet, drawing strength from his bond with Onion Boy. "We won't let you take him," he said, his voice firm despite the fear churning in his stomach.

The Master chuckled darkly, a sound that made the air feel colder. "Brave words from a child. But you have no idea what power you're dealing with."

As he spoke, shadows began to gather around him, forming into dark, menacing shapes that twisted and writhed, ready to strike. Tyler felt a shiver of dread—this wasn't like the shadow they'd faced before. This was something far more ancient, more powerful.

But Tyler squared his shoulders, his heart steady. He knew who he was now, and he knew that he and Onion Boy had defeated darkness before. He would face whatever came next, no matter how terrifying.

"We've beaten your shadow once," Tyler said, his voice unwavering. "And we'll do it again. You can't break the bond we have."

The Master's eyes narrowed, a flash of anger darkening his gaze. "We shall see, boy," he said coldly. "You've stepped into a world far beyond your understanding. This isn't over—not by a long shot."

With that, the Master turned, melting back into the shadows, his form dissolving like smoke. The clearing was silent again, but the air felt charged with his threat, an unspoken promise that he would return.

Mary placed a hand on Tyler's shoulder, her face pale but resolute. "If he comes back… we'll be ready."

Tyler nodded, his grip on the Light Amulet tightening. He looked down at Onion Boy, who glowed a determined blue, his light unwavering. They were a team, and together, they would face whatever darkness came their way.

As they left the clearing, Tyler felt a surge of determination. The journey wasn't over; it was only beginning. And with the light of friendship and courage guiding them, he knew they could withstand even the deepest shadows.

About the Author

Lance G. Jones has always dreamed of writing books and has always said that one day he would make time to do it. I can recall sitting with him as he attempted to put pen to paper to write his first book. I remember him saying that he would start with the table of contents and that once the table of contents was completed, the content would follow.

Lance, as he is known to me, has written several books, and I can say he thoroughly enjoys writing. He particularly enjoys writing children's books, as he has always been quite comical and has a wonderful childlike imagination.

Lance has also written a Christian Novel, entitled, She Went Looking for Love, which brought him to the attention of readers in many places around the globe. It was the very first book he published, which is a must-read.

Lance is also creating quite a name for himself with his *The World of Taye Tari* series. The inspiration for these stories is his grandson. There are several books in this series, with more to come.

I am sure, with the impact Lance is having, we will be hearing a lot more from this talented author in the years to come.

Stephen Jones

Made in United States
North Haven, CT
08 December 2024

60977504R00065